GW01606665

Egalitarianism:

The Metaphysical Value and Religion of our Days

Egalitarianism:

The Metaphysical Value and Religion of our days

Clergy, Nobility and People

Tradition, Family, Property Association

First edition March 2011: 1,700 copies

Tradition, Family, Property Association
P.O. Box 2713
Glasgow G62 6YJ

Tel: 0141-956-7391 Fax: 0141-956-6978
Email: info@tfpuk.org.uk

Translation from Portuguese and text preparation: Philip Moran Jr.
Editing: William Collins and Philip Moran Sr.
Design: Felipe Barandiarán

Photo opposite: "The Immaculate".
Francisco Bayeru y taller. Diocesan Seminary of Astorga, Spain

ISBN Softcover: 978-0-9568417-1-1
ISBN Hardcover: 978-0-9568417-0-4

Printed in EU

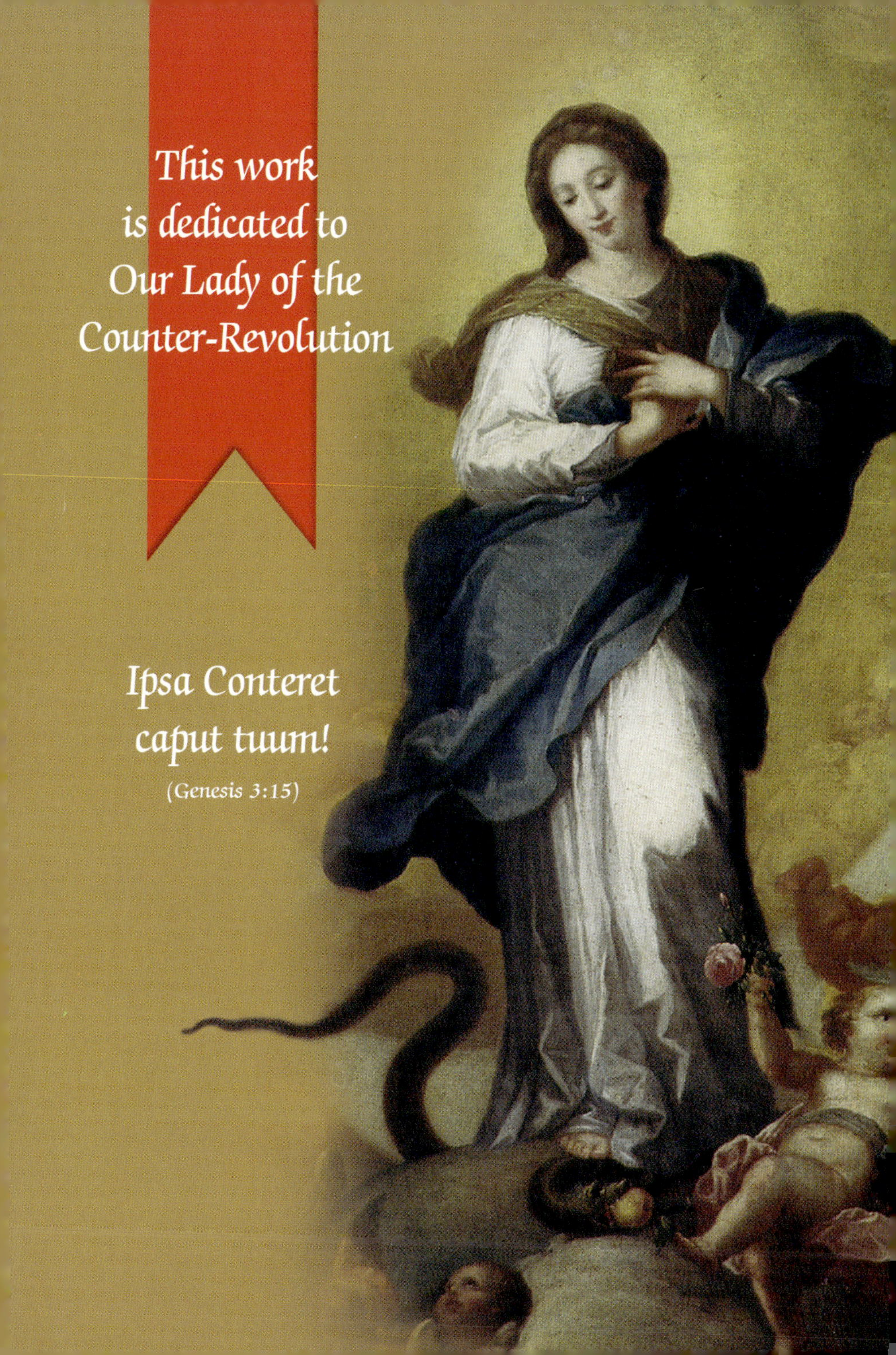

This work
is dedicated to
Our Lady of the
Counter-Revolution

Ipsa Conteret
caput tuum!
(Genesis 3:15)

Contents

FOREWORD

This present work of the eminent Catholic thinker and man of action Prof. Plinio Corrêa de Oliveira (see biography p. 69) denounces the fundamental underlying error of our days: **total equality**. In so doing he provides vital insights and arguments, without which any attempt to stem and reverse the crisis of our society will come to naught.

There is a famous moment in the life of St. Thomas Aquinas that illustrates well the importance of finding arguments. St. Thomas was having lunch with King St. Louis of France. During the conversation, forgetful of the fact that he was at the table of the king, St. Thomas began thinking about other matters. Suddenly he hit his fist on the table and said, "Ergo concluso in contra manicheus" (So much for the heresy of the Manicheans!). St. Louis immediately looked to him and asked what he was talking about. St. Thomas replied that he had found a new argument to fight the Manichean heresy.[1]

---

1) Manichæism, a religion founded by the Persian Mani in the latter half of the third century, purported to be the true synthesis of all the religious systems then known. This heresy is classified as a form of religious Dualism, since it is based on a supposed conflict between the two eternal principles of good and evil.

The discovery of a new argument caused a stir since everyone at the table was a Catholic—two were even saints—and even though all were convinced that the Manicheans were in error. Immediately orders were given to call two scribes of the royal palace to take note of the new argument so that nothing would be lost. After St. Thomas's new argument had been written down, lunch continued.

There are various picturesque aspects to this story, but I draw your attention to one in particular: the importance given to a new argument to defend a thesis already well known by all present. Why was this important? Because they were men with a profound spirit who understood that, for those who fight for the Church, the battle of ideas was more important than the battle with weapons. Since the Church expands through the propagation of ideas, the cause of the Counter-revolution does so by defending ideas. Therefore a new argument—for one who fights erroneous ideas—would be like what a new weapon is for the military.

For example, the cracking of the German Enigma code during WWII was a discovery of utmost military importance and a decisive element for the Allied victory. So also, for those who live within an ideological struggle, a new argument or insight is of the utmost importance in defending a thesis already known.

Prof. Corrêa de Oliveira, in his masterly work *Revolution and Counter-Revolution*, demonstrates that the chaos of the modern world has a cause. It is a profound cause that begets all the evils of the modern world. It has, if you will, its own personality, its own reason for being; and its name is "the Revolution".

Revolution is the name of the evil that started with Humanism and the Renaissance, passing through the French Revolution and many other evils, bringing chaos and disorder until our days. The world is being shaken and convulsed by one single Revolution. All the others to which historians give diverse names are but aspects of one single Revolution. It follows, necessarily, that this single Revolution must have an aspect related to a deformed attitude of the human spirit in a fundamental point. Once this fundamental error is made clear, one would easily understand its resulting errors.

What is this fundamental error? What is the goal of the Revolution? **It is an egalitarian movement that aims to eliminate all inequality**. By eliminating all inequality, it can establish total equality, which is total disorder. The total equality of the Revolution lies in its opposition to everything which is superior and anything which is not equal.

Sadly many people follow this egalitarian movement, whether consciously or unconsciously. It is, therefore, a duty to warn the great majority of Catholics about this movement.

This present compilation has precisely this goal and is a summary of thirteen lectures given by Prof. Corrêa de Oliveira in 1957 entitled *Egalitarianism: The Metaphysical Value and Religion of the 20th Century*. He did not have time to review them before his death in 1995, so we present them precisely as he gave them. Two other books written

Apotheosis of St. Thomas Aquinas, Zubaran (Seville)

by Prof. Corrêa de Oliveira complete the subject matter of this compilation and are highly recommended for further reading. They are: *Revolution and Counter-Revolution* (1959) and *Nobility and Traditional Analogous Elites in the Allocutions of Pope Pius XII* (1993).

A hierarchical and anti-egalitarian spirit is part and parcel of being a Catholic, as is evidenced in the writings of many popes and theologians, with special mention of St. Thomas Aquinas—upon whom Prof. Corrêa de Oliveira bases much of his argumentation. It is not without good reason that he does so:

> 1) St. Thomas Aquinas was solemnly praised in official documents by at least 70 popes throughout the centuries.
>
> 2) Pope Pius XI, in the encyclical *Studiorum ducem* (29/6/23), recalls that at the Council of Trent—convened to dispute Protestant errors—there were only two books on the altar available for consultation: The Holy Bible and the *Summa Theologica* of St. Thomas Aquinas.
>
> 3) The Code of Canon Law promulgated by Benedict XV recommended that all teaching in seminaries be done according to the method and doctrine of St. Thomas Aquinas.
>
> 4) St. Thomas, along with other saints, has the authority of a Doctor of the Church, having been made a Doctor by another saint: Pope St. Pius V.
>
> Following are some of the examples of popes praising St. Thomas Aquinas:
>
> John XXII, in the XIV century, declared, "His

doctrine is miraculous because it exceeds human capacity to take things as far as he did." He further declared, "St. Thomas Aquinas, by himself, illuminated the Church more than all the other doctors combined."

Pope Leo XIII, in his encyclical *Aternae Patris* (1789), compared St. Thomas Aquinas to a sun. "It (the *Summa*) warms the world with the splendours of its virtues and fills it with the irradiation of its doctrine."

St. Ignatius of Loyola establishes that one love and profess St. Thomas Aquinas's doctrine as one of his litmus tests of "being in consonance with the Church".

Pope Pius XI did more than all the others by making St. Thomas Aquinas a Universal Doctor of the Church.

Pope Pius XII's writings have innumerable references to St. Thomas Aquinas.

Pope Paul VI, in a Discourse given at Fossanova on 14 September 1974, the occasion of the seventh centenary of St. Thomas's death, asked himself: "Thomas, our Teacher, what lesson can you give us?" He answered with these words: "Trust in the truth of Catholic religious thought, as defended, expounded, and offered by him to the capacities of the human mind"

Pope John Paul II, in his encyclical *Fides et Ratio* (14/9/98), stated that "the Church has been justified in consistently proposing St Thomas as a master of thought and a model of the right way to do theology."

> Finally, Pope Benedict XVI extolled St. Thomas Aquinas in three General audiences in June 2010 and called the *Summa Theologica* a masterpiece.

To base one's arguments, therefore, on St. Thomas Aquinas is indisputably to argue with great authority.

In reading this short work, we hope you gain vital and constructive insights into the root cause of the crisis of our times, as well as becoming more acquainted with the late Prof. Plinio Corrêa de Oliveira who dedicated his whole life to bringing about a restoration of Christian civilisation.

Tradition, Family, Property Association

We call this process, now five centuries old, which is destroying Christian civilisation, "the Revolution". Its profound cause is an explosion of pride and sensuality that has inspired not one system, but, rather, a whole chain of ideological systems essentially egalitarian.

Introduction

The many crises shaking the world today—those of the State, family, economy, culture, and so on—are but multiple aspects of a single fundamental crisis whose field of action is man himself.

In other words, these crises have their root in the most profound problems of the soul, from whence they spread to the whole personality of present-day man and all his activities. It is, above all, a crisis of Western and Christian man, but also of other peoples to the degree that Western influence has reached and taken root among them.

We call this process, now five centuries old, which is destroying Christian civilisation, "the Revolution". Its profound cause is an explosion of pride and sensuality that has inspired not one system, but, rather, a whole chain of ideological systems essentially egalitarian.

The existence of Protestantism, of the French Revolution, and of Communism already shows a great avalanche of egalitarianism that has been inundating the world. However, in regards to the Revolution, we do not only need to show that this massive movement exists and is trying to establish a few equalities, but that there is something yet more profound.

The essence of the Revolutionary spirit is to be found in a famous document produced by the Committee of the Republic, under the Reign of Terror during the French Revolution. There, the authorities of the interior of France declared that all were invited to bring down every tower of every church and of every castle throughout France.

"Chartrain country" (detail), Alexandre Sége (1816-1885).
Museum of Fine Arts, Chartres, France

The essence of the Revolutionary spirit is to be found in a famous document produced by the Committee of the Republic, under the Reign of Terror during the French Revolution. There, the authorities of the interior of France declared that all were invited to bring down every tower of every church and of every castle throughout France. As everything was to be equal, not even buildings could be larger, one to the other. Bring down all the richer men; bring down all those who were more intelligent; suppress any aspect of material things that might give the idea of inequality.

Therefore, this egalitarian movement not only wants equality in religion, in politics, and in the economy, but also total egalitarianism in all things—not only equality among men, but also an egalitarian vision of the very universe itself. In this way man will one day see himself in a universe where all things are equal, uniform, standardised, and reduced to the same size and dimension, to the same nature and proportion. This is the essence of the Egalitarian Revolution.

What is at stake here is not insignificant. Ultimately we are dealing with an issue of aesthetics, of a love of simplicity and diversity, of a love of equality and inequality. Besides this, at a deeper level, it is a religious and moral issue as well. It is an aesthetic-moral-religious issue whose perfection is a reflection of God on earth. Herein lays the true religious battle of the 20th Century.

This religious battle is not waged, properly speaking, with dogmas or definitions of certain truths. In other words, it is not a battle waged explicitly about Revelation.

Nor is it waged between Protestants and Catholics, Left and Right, etc. These battles continue to exist, but they are secondary.

In the Roman Circus there was a primary spectacle of the great gladiators on one side locked in battle and, for variety's sake, with pygmies on the other side. Similarly one could say that our world presents much the same scenario. There is a fight of titans being waged—the one between Equality and Inequality; and then there is the other one where the dwarfs (so to speak) continue to fight about Catholicism and Protestantism, schism, dogmas, politics, etc.

I am not saying that it is not worthwhile to crush these little monsters. However, the great monster of our days is this adoration of an aesthetic-moral-religious dogma which is precisely that of inequality and variety as opposed to uniformity and equality.

Those who fight for equality do so for an aesthetic-moral-religious reason. They hate inequality because it is inequality. They love equality because it is equality. They hate diversity for diversity's sake, and love uniformity for uniformity's sake. This is a religious and moral position.

This explains the underlying cause of the religious crisis of the world today. People have adopted ways of thinking, states of spirit, and ways of living that are egalitarian. This is the religious issue of our days. Today the two opposing standards are those of Equality and Inequality.

⋆ ⋆ ⋆

One could understandably object, "But if this egalitarian movement directs all of History and transforms all the events of the world, why don't the majority of people see this, while some even deny it?"

Indeed it is important to ask why this dominating factor of our day goes unperceived, or at least is seen so incompletely as to permit it to be denied by those very same people who propagate it.

There are four principle reasons that favour this egalitarian Revolution. The first is that its adherents are directed by a levelling principle imbedded within their spirit in a subconscious manner, but not adopted by them in an entirely conscious manner. In other words, if we were to show many of the adherents of egalitarianism that they themselves think in this way, many would deny it. If anyone were to affirm to them, however, that all men should be equal in all things, they would give a slight chuckle and deny this too.

The second is that the egalitarian Revolution works very slowly through small and even insignificant transformations. Indeed the more profound transformations are the ones that are the most insignificant. It is an insidious revolution affecting the tendencies of man. Let us look at an example of a transformation which is taking place gradually at this point in time.

The necktie is a contemporary part of menswear that is dying out and something that at every moment people are looking for pretexts not to use. At an intermediate stage of the transformation we notice something very curious: people on the street with their ties half pulled off and their shirt collars unbuttoned. This represents a subconscious desire to remove the tie altogether. They do not do it only because of a lack of resolve to break with the habit of wearing a tie. If we were to present to the "egalitarian" that the study of the phenomena of the demise of the necktie had led us to the conclusion that the world is dominated by the egalitarian spirit, he would simply laugh at us.

The third reason is that it manifests itself like a strange disease that produces different symptoms in each person. Let us imagine if tomorrow São Paulo were overrun by an epidemic that produced a strange phlegm, that the onslaught of the disease was preceded by the person sneezing three times, and that the end of the disease was also preceded by three sneezes. This epidemic would become famous because it had very defined and symptomatic traits.

Imagine, though, that this epidemic produced symptoms of a different order: in one, an itch; in another, an irritation of the eyes; in yet another, a small earache; in another still, a slightly sore stomach. Each one would have a small symptom different from the other. What would be the result? The epidemic could even be more dynamic than the first, but it would go completely unnoticed.

We all need to overcome certain egalitarian tendencies, but if we were to give them free reign and then observe what they produced, we would see that the results are different in each one of us. One might want to abandon the use of the necktie. Another might want to keep the necktie and even use it correctly, but, on the other hand, he is overly friendly when he deals with his employees. A third person might treat the employees exactly how they should be treated, but he is also a teacher who likes to be a "pal" to all the students. A fourth is a teacher who is quite proper in his dealings with students, but at home is insolent to his parents because he does not accept paternal authority.

Thus, if we look at all the people infected by this disease of egalitarianism, we will see that it produces diverse symptoms in each one. So when a single cause produces different effects that are very different from one another and are very discreet, although the cause may be universal and very active, it will go unperceived. In like manner, the egalitarian revolution doesn't seek to first eliminate the necktie altogether, then the belt, then the use of socks, and so on. These things are being abandoned more or less simultaneously and, as a result, go unperceived.

Once again the superficial man infected with egalitarianism might sneer, but to the trained eye of a soldier in a war zone, slight changes in the terrain and undergrowth can indicate a booby trap.

<u>The fourth and last reason</u> that favours this egalitarian Revolution is that very few people favour total inequality. In general these are communists, leftists, and socialists. Yet we find that egalitarianism is linked to those who claim to be anticommunist or even conservative as well! So how is this?

Khrushchev once made the very curious affirmation that he didn't need to fight the West because Communism was within the West like a chick within the egg. Very true!

"Christ the King". Artist not known

The Egalitarian ideal is the reign of equality in souls and society. It is a subversion of the order God placed in the Universe. It is a subversion of the Kingship of Jesus Christ over the souls of men and human society. Its ultimate goal is the Gnostic heresy.

On the outside of this egg (the West) are written the words "Anti-Communism", but within we find the egalitarian chick of Communism.

* * *

In sum, there is a worldwide movement that has spread an ever-increasing egalitarianism over the course of centuries. It progresses with increasing velocity, since every advance feeds its acceleration. Now every movement that does not stop will arrive at its conclusion in due course. Thus this egalitarian movement will eventually destroy that which it attacks, just as the sea striking against a coastline for decades will eventually change the shape of a continent or even swallow up a whole island.

The Egalitarian ideal is the reign of equality in souls and society. It is a subversion of the order God placed in the Universe. It is a subversion of the Kingship of Jesus Christ over the souls of men and human society. Its ultimate goal is the Gnostic heresy.[2]

In the pages that follow, we will analyse the egalitarian ideal and revolution, as well as the beauty of the order God placed in the Universe that it wishes to annihilate.

---

2) For an explanation of the Gnostic Heresy see Chapter 4.

The proud person, subject to another's authority, hates first of all the particular yoke that weighs upon him. In a second phase the proud man hates all authority in general and all yokes, and, even more, the very principle of authority considered in the abstract.

Chapter 1

Equality in every field of human endevour

A Worldwide Egalitarian Movement to Establish Equality as an Ideal

The most important event of our days is that an immense egalitarian Revolution is sweeping across the whole world like a tornado sweeps across a vast plain, and it aims to establish equality as an ideal. In other words, equality as such should be established and inequality as such should be rejected.

It is a revolution—at times gradual and pacific and at others open and brutal—because it entails the transformation of a whole order of things in every imaginable aspect of life. Consequently an internal transformation within man, within the human spirit, is taking place, whereby human values are being turned inside out. It is a revolution because order is replaced by disorder.

To demonstrate this we must first consider two notions conceived as metaphysical values that express well the spirit of the Revolution. They are absolute equality and complete liberty. The two passions that serve it are pride and sensuality. For our purpose here we will focus on pride.

The proud person, subject to another's authority, hates first of all the particular yoke that weighs upon him. In a second phase the proud man hates all authority in general and all yokes, and, even more, the very principle of authority considered in the abstract. Because he hates all authority, he also hates superiority of any kind. In all this there is a true hatred for God. Consequently pride can lead to the most radical and complete egalitarianism.

This radical and metaphysical egalitarianism takes place in every possible field, and within each field, it takes place in every possible manner. Thus there is no transformation today that does not serve this egalitarian revolution. As such it is a radical violation of the natural order. Let us take a brief look at several of these fields.

Equality between men and God

Pantheism, immanentism, and all esoteric forms of religion aim to place God and men on an equal footing and to invest the latter with divine properties.

An atheist is an egalitarian who, to avoid the absurdity of affirming that man is God, commits the absurdity of declaring that God does not exist. Secularism is a form of atheism and, therefore, of egalitarianism. It affirms that it is impossible to be certain of the existence of God and, consequently, that man should act in the temporal realm as if

God did not exist; in other words, he should act like a person who has dethroned God. ★

Equality in the ecclesiastical realm

There is to be no priesthood endowed with the power of Orders, magisterium, and government, or at least a priesthood with hierarchical degrees.

Equality among the different religions

All religious discrimination is to be disdained because it violates the fundamental equality of men. Therefore the different religions must receive a rigorously equal treatment. To claim that only one religion is true to the exclusion of the others amounts to affirming superiority, contradicting evangelical meekness, and acting without tact since it closes the hearts of men against it.

Equality in the political realm

This egalitarian tenet results in the elimination, or at least the lessening, of the inequality between the rulers and the ruled. Power comes not from God but from the masses; they command and the government must obey. Monar-

---

★ Ed. note: Recent bus ads sponsored by the atheists in Britain—and backed by the British Humanist Society—confirm this first point most clearly. The ads stated, "There's probably no God, now stop worrying and enjoy your life."

chy and aristocracy are to be proscribed as intrinsically evil regimes because they are anti-egalitarian. Only democracy is legitimate, just, and evangelical.[3]

Equality in the structure of society

There must be the suppression of classes, especially those perpetuated by heredity, and the extirpation of all aristocratic influence upon the direction of society and upon the general tone of culture and customs. The natural hierarchy constituted by the superiority of intellectual over manual work will disappear through the overcoming of the distinction between them.

The abolition of the intermediate bodies

This abolition occurs both between the individual and the State, and includes the privileges inherent in every social body. No matter how much the Revolution hates the absolutism of kings, it hates intermediate bodies and the medieval organic monarchies even more. This is because monarchic absolutism tends to put all subjects, even those of the highest standing, at a level of reciprocal equality in a lower station that foreshadows the annihilation of the individual and the anonymity that have reached their apex in the great urban concentrations of socialist societies.

3) Cf. Saint Pius X, apostolic letter *Notre charge apostolique*, 25 August, 1910, American Catholic *Quarterly Review*, vol. 35 (October 1910), p. 700.

Among the intermediate groups to be abolished, the family ranks first. Until it manages to wipe it out, the Revolution tries to lower it, mutilate it, and vilify it in every way. One used to speak about the differences between families, but today families have few, if any, characteristic traits. Everything must be levelled and equalised.

Economic equality

No one owns anything; everything belongs to the collective. Private property is abolished, along with each person's right to the full fruits of his toil and to the choice of his profession.

Equality in the exterior aspects of existence

Variety easily leads to inequality of status. Therefore variety in dress, housing, furniture, habits, and so on, is reduced as much as possible.

Equality of souls

Propaganda standardises, so to speak, all souls, taking away their peculiarities and almost their own life. Even the psychological and attitudinal differences between the sexes tend to diminish as much as possible. Because of this the people—essentially a great family of different but harmonious souls united by what is common to them—disap-

"Francis I's Reception in Vienna After the Withdrawal of Napoleon's Troops". J.P. Krafft. Kunsthistorisches Museum, Vienna.

pears, and the masses, with their great, empty, collective, and enslaved souls, arise.[4]

Equality in all social relations

Here we include all forms of social relationships: between grown-ups and youngsters, employers and

4) Cf. Pius XII, Christmas broadcast, 1944, in Vincent A. Yzerman's *Major Addresses* of Pope Pius XII (St. Paul: North Central Publishing Co., 1961), vol. 2, pp. 81–82.

Most fervent support was shown [by the people of Vienna] in the reception for the Emperor, Francis I, after a devastating war and the departure of Napoleon's troops from Vienna on 20th November 1809, following an oppressive stay of six months, seven days.

employees, teachers and students, husband and wife, parents and children, etc.

Equality in the international order

The State is constituted by an independent people exercising full dominion over a territory. Sovereignty is, therefore, in public law, the image of property. Once we admit the idea of a people, whose characteristics distinguish it from other peoples, and the idea of sovereignty, we are perforce in the presence of inequalities: of capacity, virtue, number, and others. Once the idea of territory is admitted, we have quantitative and qualitative inequality among the various territorial spaces. This is why the Revolution, which is fundamentally egalitarian, dreams of merging all races, all peoples, and all states into a single race, people, and state.[5]

Equality among the different parts of a country

For the same reasons, and by analogous means, the Revolution tends to do away with any wholesome regionalism within countries today, be it political, cultural, or other.

Egalitarianism and hatred for God

Saint Thomas Aquinas teaches[6] that the diversity of creatures and their hierarchical gradation are good in themselves, for thus the perfections of the Creator shine more resplendently throughout creation. He says further that Providence instituted inequality among the angels[7] as well as

5) See *Revolution and Counter-Revolution*, Part I, Chapter 11, 3.

6) Cf. *Summa Contra Gentiles*, II, 45; *Summa Theologica*, 1, q. 47, a. 2.

7) Cf. *Summa Theologica*, 1, q. 50, a. 4.

8) Ibid., q. 96, aa. 3, 4.

9) Cf. Pius XII, Christmas broadcast, 1944, op. cit., pp. 81–82.

among men, both in the terrestrial Paradise and in this land of exile.[8] For this reason, a universe of equal creatures would be a world in which the resemblance between creatures and the Creator would have been eliminated as much as possible. To hate in principle all inequality is, then, to place oneself metaphysically against the best elements of resemblance between the Creator and creation. It is to hate God.

We will deal with this important aspect in greater detail in Chapter 3.

Limits to inequality

Of course, one cannot conclude from this doctrinal explanation that inequality is always and necessarily a good. There are limits to inequality.

All men are equal by nature and different only in their accidents. The rights they derive from the mere fact of being human are equal for all: the right to life, honour, sufficient living conditions (and therefore the right to work), property, the setting up of a family, and, above all, the knowledge and practice of the true religion. The inequalities that threaten these rights are contrary to the order of Providence. However, within these limits, the inequalities that arise from accidents such as virtue, talent, beauty, strength, family, tradition, and so forth, are just and according to the order of the universe.[9]

"The geography lesson". Albert Bettannier. Private collection

Some people do not like a professor who maintains order and hierarchy in the classroom.

CHAPTER 2

Everyday examples of egalitarian levelling

Equality and inequality in a professor

Some people do not like a professor who maintains order and hierarchy in the classroom. He is disliked because he is not the students' pal. He does not know how to be familiar, friendly, and "nice". He maintains the difference between himself and the students, and, therefore is not liked.

On the other hand, some students like a professor who shows authority and maintains a difference. They are rare, but they exist. My long experience as a professor showed me that, in general, while a student is a student he does not like a professor who shows authority. However after his student years, when recalling that time, he remembers with special sympathy those professors who knew how to maintain a hierarchy and a difference. There is a part of a student's head, even the egalitarian ones, that pays homage to inequality.

What can be said of the classroom can be said of almost anything in life.

Equality and inequality in a father of a family or a priest

There are also egalitarian or anti-egalitarian fathers of families, and even egalitarian or anti-egalitarian priests.

Today priests hardly ever use the berretta or the cassock and friars no longer use tonsures or their habit. Why? Because this makes them appear like everyone else. This is egalitarian. Unfortunately it usually does not stop there, as one can find priests using motorcycles, joking around with altar servers, and being overly familiar with both men and women in general. This is egalitarian. So everything one would expect to see in a priest, e.g. gravitas, is diluted placing him at the common level.

Unfortunately many would agree with this "loosening up" of the priest. They like to feel that the priest is just like them. However this is egalitarian and will inevitably lead to worse evils and possibly scandals. On the other hand, there are those who like when a priest embodies his sacred office and acts with dignity and propriety at all times. Here we clearly see two human types with two different mentalities.

Two families of soul: The admirers and the envious

I had the occasion to witness these two families of soul many times. This could be very clearly seen in relation to the late Cardinal Archbishop of São Paulo, Cardinal Duarte Leopoldo e Silva (d. 1938). He was very thin and upright, had a fixed gaze, well-groomed hair, and a lordly air about his whole personality.

“Sunday stroll” (1889) Ludwig Knaus. Private Collection

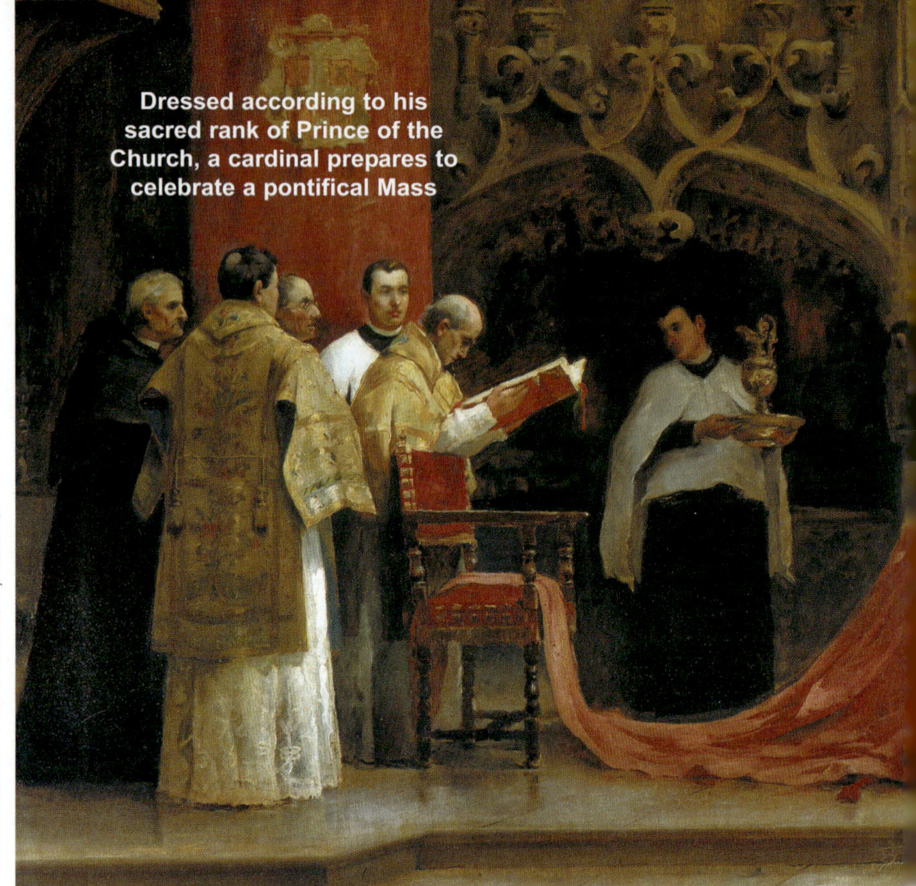

"The ponitifical Mass" Marceliano Santa Maria y Sedano (1890)
Riofrio Palace--Prado Museum, Madrid.

When the Cardinal left the church, people frequently would come up to kiss his hand, as was the custom. I noticed there were two distinct families of souls irrespective of social class.

Some would approach him enchanted with his superiority and kiss the ring on his finger, content to pay him this homage. He would say a few words and they would leave as if having received a precious gift.

Others approached him only because he was passing by and were possessed of the sort of stupid fear of one who

in reality is envious and begrudges the fact he has to do this. They would leave in a state of anger.

Here we clearly have two distinct families of souls: one that likes equality and another that likes inequality.

Equality and self-respect

There are also two different types of people. The first type is self-respecting individuals who present themselves and expect to be respected. They let their particular gifts shine forth with a natural superiority.

The second type of person has little self-respect and behaves in a pseudo-natural style. They smile, are very easy going, think nothing is wrong, and treat everyone with no reserve.

Equality and height

It is interesting to observe that, as the egalitarian revolution progresses, furniture tends to become lower in height. When we sat down on furniture made decades ago—even common household furniture—we could feel they were made for people who understood their inherent dignity as a human being. They are not level with the ground, they have high backs, and sometimes do not have armrests. As the egalitarian movement becomes more accentuated, furniture tends to become lower and is built in a way that a person sinks into it and sprawls. One could easily begin an endless debate on the merits or demerits of this, but what we are showing here is how this fits in with innumerable other tendencies along the same line.

The same thing happens with tall buildings such as skyscrapers. The height of the ceiling tends to become lower compared to older buildings. Everything becomes standardised and cramped. Many pseudo-practical reasons could be given for this to be, but again we merely point out the tendency.

Science tends to crush man so he is no longer king of God's creation

It is very interesting to observe how science presents our universe to the non-scientific person. We know that

God created the universe with everything in harmony and proportion with varying degrees over which man was to reign as sovereign. Now general science is taught in a way that man feels like an ant in face of these fabulous distances, sizes, masses, etc. It tends to make him incapable of understanding his own worth, his own sovereignty in relation to this universe, and gives him a strange sensation of being totally equal to everyone else.

For example if we take ten men and place them at the foot of the Himalayas, it is a bit meaningless for them to argue who is taller because the Himalayas crush them with their sheer massiveness. A man feels flattened, just as in the enormous urban centres today.

The same happens when considering the universe from the opposite spectrum of microorganisms. Science shows us what is immensely small not just for us to marvel at the works of the Creator, but rather with a tendency to make us feel out of our depth. Again our sovereignty over the universe is shaken and we are made to feel insignificant.

Both the macro and micro visions of the universe, as shown by science today to the common person, tend to create an egalitarian spirit.

Very little or no emphasis on the inequality of souls

Souls are even more profoundly different one from another than the physical character of man. How very interesting it is to observe the differences in souls. Even within the same family or family of souls where the souls are moved by

Robert Nanteuil. Carnavalet Museum, Paris.

Henri de la Tour d'Auvergne, Viscount of Turenne

the same spirit, the same mentality, they are, notwithstanding, so very different one from the other in temperament and in everything else. That is a real treasure.

Let us take the example of two French generals of the 17th century. Henri de la Tour d'Auvergne, Viscount of Turenne, was a general who made his plans very methodically and would apply them methodically and with a great deal of care. Louis, Prince of Condé, was a general who acted on the spur of the moment. He never made plans. He had a tremendous nose like a bird or fox that seemed to give him the ability as if to smell out the situation. Arriving at the battlefield, he would cast a cursory glance and then decide what was to be done. This difference between the two generals delighted the men of the time and was commented on by them in every way.

Today few find it interesting to appreciate souls and to comment on their differences (are there even any interesting souls on which to comment?). No one sees the beauty in the variety of souls. Why? It is because this was removed from our mental horizons.

In this age of materialism, the soul, which is superior to the body, is undervalued. The problems of the soul are mostly dealt with on the psychiatrist's couch. The value of the spirit is reduced to the minimum and put on the same level as the material.

The Duke d’Enghien, the future Great Condé, victor over the Spanish troops in the battle of Rocroi in 1643. (F-J. Heim, Versailles Museum)

The egalitarian spirit tends to eliminate everything to do with respect and courtesy of manners between genders and age groups

"Boat excursion" Emanuel Phillip Fox. Art Gallery of New South Wales, Sidney

Equality of sexes and ages

There are certain inequalities that come from nature itself, such as one's gender. Inequality of gender exists so there may be procreation. This in turn creates the distinction between parent and child.

Today these differences are all minimised. Of course, they cannot deny the difference between sexes, but everything is done to equalise the difference as much as possible. The same goes for the difference of age. Woman is equal to man, the child to the parent, the youngster to the mature adult, etc. Everything is done so that people are as equal as possible.

The body is overvalued and the intellect undervalued

Everything having to do with sports, health, and nutrition is given much more importance than to what is derived from the intellect. One hears very little praise about someone's intelligence compared to the praise heaped on someone's physical capabilities. Also gone are the days when one's head was more important than one's feet. As a result, dignified headwear is out and extravagant footwear is in.

Although everyone recognises the superiority of intellectual work over manual labour, no one praises it. For example one rarely hears a commentary like this: "Impressive! I saw 5,000 workers struggling with a certain project.

Then the engineer came along and with a quick review streamlined the project. Everything changed. How marvellous is intellectual work!" Sadly one rather hears something like, "Poor manual worker, how he works so hard."

I once heard someone in a Catholic school speaking about the unskilled workers saying that we need to raise their salaries. Not too long afterwards, when speaking about raising the salaries of the teachers, the same person said, "Look, we have many teachers and we will pay them what we like. We don't need to give them a raise."

Why do we speak about the poor workers and not about the poor teacher? This is because of the nobility of intellectual work, and no one wants to speak of that.

"Nostalgia". Almeida Junior (1899)
Pinocotheca of the State
of São Paulo (Brazil)

Vulgarisation of language

Beautiful literary forms, eloquent speeches, and dignified everyday language are in fast decline. One used to say, "She blushed," but today it is more common to say, "She turned red." To blush is a mental phenomenon that is reflected physically. To become red is something purely physical that could as easily happen to one's hand. *

Egalitarianism in the diplomatic sphere

Let us speak about embassies. At the head of the embassy we have the ambassador. Generally he is serious, cultured, and lives in an appropriate house to represent the nation. Under him are the various employees, among whom are the attachés and even spies.

If we make a test to see what interests people more today, we will find that it is undoubtedly the work of the

* Ed. note: Emails, texting, and tweeting have all contributed to the vulgarising and equalising of language.

spy. If someone were to pass by a bookshop window and see a book entitled "The Memoirs of an Ambassador from the Court of Saint James" and another entitled "The Memoirs of a British Spy", it is obvious which one would be the bestseller.

The ambassador is considered as an ornament on a wedding cake and not as the key element of the embassy. It is the spy, or the commercial or military attaché, who is considered the most useful.

Differences between cities and families disappear

The illustrious past of cities and towns also tends to be forgotten as a result of this equalising trend. The reason for their names and emblems tend to be barely remembered.

One used to speak about the differences between families, but today families have few, if any, characteristic traits. Everything must be levelled and equalised.

* * *

We could multiply the examples almost infinitely to show that it is not only inequality between men that our century hates, but also every type of inequality in every field. It hates inequality in nature, in the diversity in men, in the diversity of plants, and in virtually everything.

Thus the Egalitarian Revolution clearly shows itself to be a philosophical and religious revolution that hates something intrinsic to the Universe. The Universe is full of inequalities and the Revolution hates them. Everything that exists must be transformed to fit into an egalitarian concept of life. Those that perchance cannot be transformed are rejected, destroyed, or consigned to oblivion. In this way Equality as a value reigns supreme.

So the question arises: Is inequality in the Universe a good or an evil? We will look at this next.

"Creation". The Nuremberg Bible (1493)

Inequality exists as an excellence of the Universe. It is through inequalities that God better manifests Himself to man.

CHAPTER 3

Teaching of the Catholic Church Regarding Inequality

Prof. Corrêa de Oliveira dedicates six of his thirteen lectures to the Catholic Church's teaching on inequality. It would unnecessarily extend the present work if we were to reproduce all six lectures. Instead we will reproduce the one we consider sufficient to prove his thesis. However in order to show our reader the depth and breadth of his argument, we list the subjects dealt with in the other lectures:

- Justification of inequality based on the hierarchies God established in the Universe: the angelic choirs
- God's government and providence of the Universe through secondary creatures and secondary causes
- The organisation of the State and society analogous to that of the angelic choirs
- Why God created many creatures and not only one; the intrinsic goodness of variety

⋆ ⋆ ⋆

At this point we need to ask: What does the Catholic religion think of the doctrine of equality? I will deal with three main aspects of this question, which can be summarised as follows:

1) The Catholic Church affirms that God created the Universe with inequalities, in fact, enormous inequalities. God is the author of these inequalities.

2) These inequalities are not a consequence of Original Sin. They are not some sort of disfigurement introduced into the Universe because of sin. Much to the contrary, inequality exists as an excellence of the Universe, as a refinement of the perfection of the Universe.

3) Why is it a refinement of the perfection of the Universe? As St. Thomas Aquinas proves, especially in the *Suma contra Gentiles* (Book II, Chapter 45), it is through inequalities that God better manifests Himself to man. It is precisely because inequality exists in the Universe that its likeness to God shines brighter for man, and it is because of this more perfect likeness of God that equality is a good in itself.

Let us deal with these points in more depth.

Why is inequality in Creation a good

St. Thomas first asks whether it is good that there are many creatures and not only one creature. Then there

"Paradise"
Giusto dei Menabuoi
Baptismal font in Padua,
Italy

Another example is a craftsman and his work. He conceives a project. It will be perfect to the degree it corresponds to what was conceived

is a second question as to whether they all should be equal or unequal amongst themselves.

To the latter question St. Thomas responds that inequality is a good. God made inequality in the universe as a perfection of the universe. Furthermore, the greater the number of inequalities, the greater perfection there will be in a specific ensemble of things.

Thus the inequality of creation is a good in itself. Since this good exists in itself, it is also better that it exist in the works of man than for it not to exist.

Let us see how St. Thomas proves this.

The Universe should resemble God

First he shows that inequality in Creation is a good, considering God as the agent and the universe as the effect. In this relation of cause and effect he shows that it is more perfect to have unequal creatures. He takes the following presupposition as his starting point: Creation should bear the likeness of God.

Every agent intends to introduce its likeness into its effect, in the measure that its effect can receive it. Let us take a professor as an example who tends to introduce his likeness in the effect, who is his student. He tends to give the student a knowledge that is like his own. His classes will be good, that is they will be an efficient cause, in the measure that the effect resembles the cause; in other words, in the measure that the knowledge acquired by the student resembles the professor's.

Another example is a craftsman and his work. He conceives a project. It will be perfect to the degree it corresponds to what was conceived. The same applies to a musician and his compositions; or to an engineer and a house he builds. The musician has a specific idea and composes a piece of music to express what was in his spirit. The music will be good in the measure that it expresses the harmony the musician intended.

So the idea is that if an agent acts well, then the effect resembles the cause. The more perfect the cause, the more the effect will resemble it. The better the professor is, the better will be the effect; the better the musician is, the more perfect the harmony will be, etc.

Therefore since God is most perfect, it follows that the universe also be most perfect. By "most perfect" we do not mean that it has the greatest perfection possible, but that it has a high degree of perfection. In order for the Universe to have this high degree of perfection, it follows naturally that it bear a great likeness to God, since the perfection of the effect lies in its likeness to the cause. In this way is proven that the perfection of the Universe consists in its likeness to God.

Creatures cannot have a perfect likeness to God, only a partial one

St. Thomas continues by saying that there are two types of relationship between cause and effect. Sometimes the effect is of the same species as the cause as, for example, a flame lights another flame. The second flame has a perfect likeness to the first because, as the cause and effect are of the same species, there is a perfect likeness between cause and effect.

However when the cause and effect are of different species, the likeness is not the same—for example, Donato Bramante designed St. Peter's Basilica. There is not a perfect likeness between Bramante and the basilica as there is between one table and another table. Bramante made a plan, but the basilica is not of the same species as man. When the cause and effect are of different natures, the effect is always of an inferior species to the cause and, because of this, cannot have all the qualities of the cause. What is inferior cannot contain all the qualities of what is superior.

God is more perfectly represented in the multiplicity and variety of species

Thus far we have two points:

1) The Universe should bear God's likeness.

2) Things created by God cannot have a perfect likeness to Him, only a partial one.

Hence St. Thomas says all things created are of a different species from God. If they are of an inferior species, none individually can attain to a perfect likeness to God and represent Him entirely.

As a result the more species that are created, the more perfect is God represented. Consequently several species of

"Creation of the Universe"
Jan Brueghel II
Prado Museum, Madrid

creatures represent God more perfectly than only one species of creature.

St. Thomas says that the species are always different from each other. So what is a species? In common language, for example, an angel is a species. Man is another species.

Irrational beings are another species. In these examples we have pure spirit, spirit plus matter, and then matter only. It is clear that these three species cannot be equal amongst themselves. Species are like numbers. If I remove or add one attribute from a species, it becomes another species. For example, let us take the number "7". If I subtract one, it becomes "6" and if I add one it becomes "8".

So there have to be several species and these species have to be unequal. From this, one concludes that inequality is a means that exists so the Universe resembles God more perfectly.

Let us give an example within our own species, i.e., Man. Michelangelo had the capacity to build, sculpt, and paint. He was capable of making three categories of works of art. He gave a much more complete demonstration of his character by producing works of art in three different categories than by producing art in only one category. This is because in him existed, as a cause, all these predicates. In a painting alone, he could not express everything that was expressed in the other forms of art.

Therefore inequality in creation is a good

From the above it has been proven that, given the relationship of cause and effect, inequality in creation is a good. Inequality is a good in what God created, and it is also a good in man's creations because they are extensions of the works of God. Dante said very appropriately that the works of man are God's grandchildren. God is the father of man, and man is father of his own works.

A greater inequality in creatures manifests a greater capacity of the Creator

Let us take a look at the following reasoning. When a person has the capacity for many acts and only performs some of them, his capacity has not been entirely actualised. In other words, something has not been expressed. Imagine a man who has the capacity to be a great orator making extraordinary speeches. However along comes a war and he is shot in the tongue. As a result his oratorical expression is curtailed. He still has oratorical capacity. He can even imagine the magnificent speeches he could give and even write, but he can no longer deliver them because his capacity of expression has been curtailed almost entirely. His potentiality to say certain things in certain circumstances is actualised in an incomplete manner.

St. Thomas reminds us that the effect is all the more perfect in the measure that the agent fully actualises his potentialities.

Consider a painter who has the capacity to produce a painting with physiognomic expressions. This painting will be more perfect in the measure that there are more faces, because in this way he expresses his pictorial capacity more than if he only painted one face.

"The Last Supper" by Leonardo da Vinci

Let us analyse Leonardo da Vinci's famous "The Last Supper" in Milan. In "The Last Supper" he represents twelve Apostles, twelve faces, and twelve states of spirit and temperamental reactions in face of a horrible revelation. These were people who had abandoned everything to follow Our Lord. They were in a closed room at a very intimate moment when they heard Our Lord say, "One of you will betray Me." Two sentiments will immediately arise: First, who is it? Second, is it that one in whom I noticed such and such a thing?

Of course in face of such a revelation, the reactions will be lively and so he paints twelve temperaments reacting in different ways to a single psychological situation. Da Vinci had the capacity to paint twelve Apostles in twelve different ways.

"The Last Supper" (1495-1498) Leonardo da Vinci Santa Maria delle Grazie, Milan

If, instead, he had done a painting of St. Peter hearing the words, "You will betray me," the painting would be less perfect, because the capacity he showed in painting the twelve was actualised. Until it became an act, it would be unfulfilled.

The "Council of Trent" by Titian

I have a print of a picture attributed to Titian representing the Council of Trent. He did not make his picture by reproducing all the faces of the 400 bishops present, but instead sketched their backs, as well as the altar, some books, and the back of the Church. How did he make the picture come alive? He painted the 400 heads from the back, but in conversation one with the other. It is so fantastic that when you look at the picture, it seems perfectly natural and as if he did this without much effort.

"Council of Trent" Titian. Louvre Museum, Paris

So here we have a man capable of doing such a work. He did not only have talent, but also a great patience to sketch 400 heads. By sketching 400 heads and not only one, his capacity was more fully actualised, and in this lies the value of the picture.

The more power God manifests in creating different creatures, the more perfect creation is

Continuing the reasoning, God has an infinite power in the Universe. The more God exercises His power in creating the Universe, the more perfect the Universe will be. If, by sketching 400 heads and not only one, Titan's picture became more perfect, likewise, God does something more perfect if He were to create 400 beings instead of only one.

Now God does not only have the power to create beings, but also has the power to create beings in different degrees. Therefore the more degrees He places in creation, the more He exercises His power to create degrees and the more perfect creation becomes.

Inequality amongst men: A cascade of goodness

This argument, which is valid when speaking of God or an artist, can also be applied to a people. A people that engenders a great number of social classes in its political and social organisation that are highly proportionate is, by the same reasoning, accomplishing a more complete work than if it only produced one social class.

This is why the European nobility, constituted of various noble classes, engendered something much more perfect than if it had only produced one noble class in which all were equal. As St. Thomas affirms, there would not be a perfect likeness of God in the universe if all things were of one grade of being.

He further states that the creature is more perfect to God's likeness in the measure that it is not only good, but also acts for the good of other things. No creature can act for the benefit of another, however, unless there are both many and unequal created things.

Therefore it is good that inequality exists so that there are people to whom things can be given. This argument destroys a central argument of the Revolution that anyone in need is to be pitied and everyone who receives a favour is humiliated. This is false. It is in the economy of Divine Providence that some men receive from others.

Whence we conclude: if I see a very unequal society, I can affirm that it is beautiful since each man reflects God in relation to those under him. It is a cascade of goodness.[10]

An ensemble of finite beings is more than only one finite being

Imagine God had created some other world that was much more excellent than this world of ours, but where there was only one creature with much greater qualities than we see here. St. Thomas says that a creature is finite, that a finite creature has a finite goodness, and a finite goodness is always less than one finite goodness added to another. So if there is a more excellent world, it is always better to also have something else.

---

10) For more on this, cfr. *Nobility and Analogous Traditional Elites in the Allocutions of Pius XII*, Appendix IV: "Forms of Government in the Light of the Church's Social Doctrine", and also Document V: "The Church's Doctrine on Social Inequalities".

We could exemplify this as follows. Take stone and water. A stone has several unique qualities, as does water. No one will deny this. It is a radical impossibility to make something both stone and water at the same time. In the created world something is either a stone or it is water. This is because every contingent being can only possess a certain number of perfections.

Take two men. One cannot imagine one person being at the same time a great lawyer, a great doctor, and a great academic, because he will end up by being none of these things. Human capacity of itself is limited, and a man can only have a certain number of perfections. Either a man is a great general or he is a great philosopher, but a general-philosopher is a contradiction of terms.

Many unequal creatures better represent the infinite Divine understanding and power

God understands many things. Understanding is received by a being according to the understanding of each being. Since God understands many things, it is proper that He create many things so that His cognitive potentiality is actualised. For this reason it is proper that many things exist in the Universe. Now since God understands many things that are unequal, it is proper that He created many things unequally. Unequal things better represent the perfection of the understanding of God.

The same can be said in relation to the will. The power of God is to create many things. Therefore the more things

A people that engenders a great number of social classes in its political and social organisation that are highly proportionate is, by the same reasoning, accomplishing a more complete work than if it only produced one social class.

"The Estates-General assembled by Louis XIII at the

He creates, the more perfectly is His power actualised and the more perfect is Creation. Since He has the power to create things in different degrees, it is proper that He create different degrees. The diversity of degrees is another excellence of the Universe.

The work of a great artist should be excellent in the relationship amongst its parts; for this to be, the parts need to be unequal

It is proper for a great artist to have a great perfection. In the work of a great artist one does not distinguish between the perfection of the parts and the perfection of the relationship that the artist establishes amongst the various parts.

Take for example the artist who made the Parthenon in Athens. Each one of those parts, let's say the columns, is very beautiful. Each one of the columns is excellent. In the colonnade the first perfection we see lies in the excellence of the all the columns together. There is a second perfection, however, that does not lie in the excellence of each column considered individually, but rather in the relationship of the columns amongst themselves and in the whole edifice of which they are part.

A musical composition is another example. We have the beauty of each note and the relationship of each note amongst themselves to form the melody.

There are then two types of perfections: the intrinsic perfection of each part and the perfection of the relationships that unite these parts to make an excellent whole.

St. Thomas says that in every being we should distinguish between the excellence of the parts and the excellence of the relationships amongst the parts to form a whole. The excellence of the whole is greater than the excellence of its parts. For the whole to be harmonious, it is necessary that the parts be unequal. Because where there is equality there can be no harmony, there can be no ordering of the different parts in an adequate way. Therefore for the perfection of the whole it is proper that the parts be unequal.

Thus when we see inequality in a whole, this inequality is not for the benefit of that which is superior, but benefits each one of the parts of this whole. Likewise, when I see a political or social organisation that is unequal, I should not think that this inequality is the sole privilege of those on top, but rather that the inequality is a privilege of the whole. It is in the interest of the whole that this inequality exists.

Hence this modern concept that inequality of wealth only benefits the rich, that social inequality only benefits the nobles, that the inequality within the Catholic Church between clergy and laity only benefits the clergy, all this is a lie. It is the whole of the Church, it is the whole of civil society that benefits from this. Those who are inferior also benefit from this inequality.

★ ★ ★

From all of the above we can conclude that to wish to destroy inequality in the Universe is to wish to destroy what it has that is more excellent: what is more Godlike (I would dare to say) and where God is more perfectly reflected. Now to hate that which reflects God most excellently is to hate God Himself; thus it is entirely evident that the egalitarian Revolution is against God.

Quis ut Deus!

"I will put enmities between you and the woman, and your seed and her seed: she shall crush your head, and you shall lie in wait for her heel."

(Genesis 3:15)

CHAPTER 4

The Egalitarian Revolution: A diabolic conspiracy to lead men to the Gnostic heresy

Generally speaking, the authors that deal with egalitarian revolutionary forces do so in light of Divine Providence. They try to study, within the plans of Divine Providence, why God would permit such a conspiracy to actually attain its end. They also treat—albeit less profoundly—of another matter: What is the Devil's ultimate intention with this?

We must never loose sight of the fact that, although the government of the whole universe and of all creatures belongs to God, He gave men free-will and endowed the angels with intelligence and will. The Devil, in spite of having been cast into Hell, still has his angelic intelligence and will.

So it is reasonable for us to try to understand, using the intellectual elements at our disposal, why the Devil wants such a conspiracy. Furthermore, given that the Devil is the driving force behind this conspiracy, it is of capital importance for us to know what his final goal is.

Gnosis necessarily has to be the final goal of this conspiracy of the Devil. As a logical and ineluctable consequence of circumstances in which he finds himself, he has to want humanity to be Gnostic. His interest is not that mankind fall into just any heresy; it has to be the Gnostic heresy.

In simple terms, the Gnostic heresy is a doctrine radically opposed to the laws that God placed in the Universe, because they represent His likeness. It aims, therefore, to make the Universe the opposite of God's likeness as much as possible. Ultimately, it aims at the destruction of being itself, which we will deal with later. To accomplish this, the Gnostic heresy's most dynamic element is egalitarianism.

To understand the reason for this, we must first address some presuppositions. For greater clarity, we will speak anthropomorphically, that is, attributing a human personality to the Devil.

The Devil is an angel, a defeated angel who finds himself in a highly contradictory position with himself. He is, properly speaking, a contradiction, a failure, the one who has been defeated and crushed. God cast him from his exalted throne into the abyss of Hell. There he continues to exist, and his first contradiction is that he knows God is God and thus worthy of all homage and adoration. As a result of a disordered love of himself, however, he does not want to pay this homage. Therefore, even if God were to permit the Devil to adore Him, he would not want to do so. The Devil is in Hell of his own free will because he does not want to accept a crystal clear reality. His will is fixed in evil. He hates God and wants nothing to do with Him.

A being in such a situation is completely twisted. It has deviated from its true and proper end and now pursues an end it knows is wrong. The Devil knows he does not deserve to be adored, but he nonetheless wants it. So there is a tremendous contradiction within the Devil.

It is in the light of this contradiction that we will find an explanation for the Devil's plan regarding this universal conspiratorial movement. Why does a being placed in such a contradictory position desire such a heresy and devise a plan as a result?

Example of the bankrupt Japanese man: Everything is lost. What is left for me to do?

I will continue to speak anthropomorphically. Let us imagine an individual who is suffering. I remember there was a Japanese man who owned the house I rented on Santa Efigenia Street. His finances were in a bad state and he was on the verge of declaring bankruptcy when a fire broke out in his house. Seeing everything he had going up in flames, he realised he could be accused of arson and attempting to declare a fraudulent bankruptcy, so that in addition to the disgrace of bankruptcy, he might end up in jail. In view of this situation, he entered the burning house and tried to save some of his belongings. While so doing, the ceiling fell upon him, burning him quite badly. He ended up in hospital in a miserable state.

Now picture the case of this Japanese man convalescing in hospital with his finances in ruins. While recovering, he would reflect as any individual who has suffered a disaster would: "Everything is lost. What can I do?" No matter how little is left, he will still think about what can be done.

How to spend eternity?

Similarly, this is what happened with the Devil. He revolted against God and was cast into disgrace, so the Devil did the same as the Japanese man: "I have eternity before me. What shall I do during eternity?" Naturally his solution would first require making a survey of his situation:

1) "The first thing that I have left is my existence. The second thing is my angelic nature. I have made myself a reprobate. I have made myself an evil being, eternally unhappy, but I continue to be an angel, and I continue to have all the lucidity and power inherent to an angelic nature. Third, I have a certain freedom of movement.

Furthermore, I can increase this liberty of movement by multiplying the sins committed by mankind." When the sins of men increase, God grants the Devil greater possibility to tempt them. In this way the Devil can manage to increase his liberty of movement.

2) "On the other hand, God's work contains something which could be called a weak point: mankind. I can do nothing against the angels. They are already confirmed

in grace; they can no longer sin. To do evil to inanimate creation is of some interest, but not as much as using all my intelligence and will against mankind, the weak point in Creation. Mankind is a weak point because it is in crisis. It is a weak point because it is that part of Creation which I can cause to be lost! I will use all the means at my disposal and cast myself upon it for its perdition."

3) The Devil might think, however, "What does it profit me to disturb the work of God?" From a certain point of view, it could be considered a failure for the Devil because he cannot eliminate God nor can he harm God's intrinsic glory—the glory God gives to Himself. As for His extrinsic glory—the glory creatures give to God—He receives that from Hell as well, because it glorifies Him in His justice. So even through sin does the Devil end up by giving glory to God.

Therefore everything that the Devil does against God ends up being for the greater glory of God. This being the case, to what purpose does the Devil insult God?

There is a French proverb that says, "Insult the sun, and it will shine all the same." The Devil knows quite well that it is the same with God, and that he is doing a very bad action that reflects the eternal and inexorable disorder in which he finds himself.

It is a bit like something I once saw on a train at a stop on the way to the coastal town of Santos. A few passengers got off the train and teased some young lads nearby. Those young boys were annoyed and grumbled amongst themselves as the passengers re-boarded the train. When the

"Theophilus pays homage to the Devil, but soon repents and the Virgin appears to him."
Psalter of Paris, Condé Museum, Chantilly

The Devil's main focus is to cause as many men as possible to go to hell, to cause man not to perceive the good things God placed on earth in Creation so he will not be edified and sanctified thereby, and to stop man from completing the beauty of creation with his own work.

train started to move, the lads threw a volley of stones at it knowing full well they would not damage it or anyone inside. They knew it was a futile manifestation of hatred, but their desire to manifest what was inside of them led them to perform that action. It is a form of useless protest that represents well the Devil's state of spirit.

The Devil's intention: "Ad maiorem Dei injuriam"

Even though he knows he can do nothing against God, the Devil wants to do the opposite of the work of God in that part of Creation that can still be changed, which is mankind. Thus his intention is to counter the work of God in men, to take the greatest number of men to Hell, and to cause those men who do go to heaven to be less holy than they could have been. He also desires, in some way, to disfigure material creation in the measure that it gives glory to God. All of these actions are done to pursue the Devil's motto: *ad maiorem Dei injuriam* (for the greater insult to God).

Since this is the Devil's position towards God, we can conclude that two things are of interest to the Devil: first, man; second, material creation.

The Devil's main focus is to cause as many men as possible to go to hell, to cause man not to perceive the good things God placed on earth in Creation so he will not be edified and sanctified thereby, and to stop man from completing the beauty of creation with his own work. If he were able, he would even destroy something God made. However the material creation is much less important to him. What the Devil really wants are men's souls, which are precisely the centre of the battle.

The Devil wants to eliminate the beauty of material creation to help take souls to Hell

Notwithstanding, one of the things which the Devil strives to do to influence souls is to present a vision of the universe where variety and inequality, the most striking elements God placed in the universe to reflect His Likeness, are not perceived. God imprinted His Likeness upon the Universe so that souls might be saved. In removing that likeness of the Universe from the human field of vision, the Devil removes something that does good to souls and, as a result, places their eternal salvation in jeopardy. Thus the Devil strives to present the most uniform and egalitarian culture possible.

Since every form of variety in human life—whether in institutions, laws, or ambiences—naturally leads to sanctification, the Devil aims to influence every aspect of human life with this principle of uniformity. By eliminating all this and establishing uniformity and egalitarianism, the likeness of God is erased.

In sum, a uniform and egalitarian cultural panorama must be established because variety and inequality are reflections of God.

The Devil's ultimate goal: To destroy being itself

The Devil would not only like to present man with a cultural vision that destroyed variety and hierarchy as much as possible, but also one that destroyed the very concept of being.

He cannot, absolutely speaking, destroy being because he does not have the power to do so. For example, he cannot stop a table from existing. He can certainly cause a man to lose his soul, but he cannot destroy the soul; he cannot eliminate being as such.

Nonetheless, the Devil is not just satisfied with reducing God's Creation to ruins, nor is he satisfied with just fighting for uniformity and against hierarchy. He wants to completely scramble the very concept of being in the human mind. He wants to implement a state of nothingness, to reabsorb creation into the primitive nothingness. This is Gnosis, properly speaking. If he succeeds, he will have attained his ultimate goal.

Solemn meeting room designed by Prof. Plinio Corrêa de Oliveira

"If the Revolution is disorder, the Counter-Revolution is the restoration of order. And by order we mean the peace of Christ in the Reign of Christ, that is, Christian civilisation, austere and hierarchical, fundamentally sacral, antiegalitarian, and antiliberal."

***Revolution and Counter-Revolution*, Part II, Chapter 2,1**

Chapter 5

The attitude of a true Catholic vis-à-vis the Egalitarian Revolution

To conclude this presentation of Prof Corrêa de Oliveira's series of thirteen lectures, we will make use of his summing-up, as well as his comments on what the attitude of a true Catholic today should be vis-à-vis the Egalitarian Revolution.

⋆ ⋆ ⋆

Thus far we have demonstrated the three main points of our topic:

1) An egalitarian Revolution exists in the world. It directs the course of events in order to establish equality as a supreme ideal—at times gradual and pacific, and at others fast and brutal. As such, it is an aesthetic-moral-religious revolution directed against God's likeness in Creation and, therefore, against God Himself.

2) How variety and inequality are inherent qualities of God's Creation in order that it be more perfectly in His Likeness. God organised the universe with three orders: the angels, who are pure spirit; men, who are both spirit and matter; and purely material beings. God also placed an enormous number of other categories within each one of

these Orders. God created beings both unequal and various for usefulness and philosophical and theological character.

3) The final goal of this Egalitarian Revolution is to create a culture and human order that subverts true culture and order, leading to man's perdition. It is the Devil's deceitful and ultimately unsuccessful conspiracy to combat the plans of Providence with the intention to lead mankind to total disorder and the Gnostic heresy.

* * *

To face this great historical phenomenon of the Egalitarian Revolution and its diametric opposition the Catholic Church's teaching regarding variety and hierarchy, there are two types of positions to take: the fervent Catholic and the lukewarm Catholic.

Characteristics of a fervent Catholic

What are the characteristics of a fervent Catholic?

1) A fervent Catholic must have, above all, the disposition to abandon everything that is opposed to the Catholic Faith. Without this disposition one can never be a fervent Catholic.

2) One needs to be convinced that all things need to be arranged according to the principles and interests of the Church.

3) One must be convinced that the doctrine and interests of the Church should never be sacrificed for anything. Therefore no one should ever demand that the Church change them for any reason. The Church is the rule and measure of all things. This is corollary to rule no. 2.

4) One should only find people and things agreeable to the degree that they are imbued with the spirit of the Church. This is one of the most important characteristics of a true Catholic. If I meet a person that does not have the Catholic spirit and I find his company simply delightful, this should immediately set off alarm bells in me. I should say to myself, "My subconscious is profoundly intoxicated, because I found pleasure in someone or something that is not Catholic." This alarm bell should immediately ring in my conscious. Why? Because this attraction reveals something in me that is not Catholic.

5) Finally one should totally reject or, at least, give the cold shoulder to all that opposes the Church. The true Catholic is intransigent! If there is something that is opposed to the Church, he rejects it completely. If, for some reason of the moment, to avoid a greater evil, or for some other reason he cannot effectuate this complete rejection, he penalises it by giving it the cold shoulder.

Characteristics of lukewarm Catholics

What are the characteristics of a lukewarm Catholic?

1) A person only refrains from professing express error, e.g., he does not become Protestant. As for the rest, he goes along with it all the way. The best example of this is Brazil, where Protestant propaganda obtains no results, where no one changes his religion, yet no one takes seriously the religion he has. People simply follow the Catholic religion out of habit because it would be too shocking or hard to break with all their habits. This is tepidity at its

most scandalous. These are precisely the people about whom Our Lord was speaking when He said, "If you were either hot or cold I would judge you, but because you are lukewarm I will vomit you from my mouth."

Splendour and hierarchy: Papal procession within St. Peter's Basilica in 1920.

2) One only fights the errors and the vices that Public Opinion finds excessive. This is especially characteristic of the lukewarm Catholic. For instance, let us say there is a scandal in the city and everyone deplores it. The tepid

Catholic will say, "One is sorely tempted to worry about the future of humanity. Thank God His Providence still helps us." However if public opinion doesn't take notice, neither does he.

3) He has the tendency to adapt himself to everything, to every circumstance, to all things. For this reason when it is the fashion to wear short sleeves, he thinks it is fine, and, only if the sleeves were shorter than the fashion permits, would it be wrong. When the clothes people generally use begin to expose the person's back with simply a strap on each shoulder, he says, "It's understandable. We have to follow the style; we can't live in the past." He thinks, "It's really not so bad. After all, we shouldn't speak badly of others." If almost complete nudity becomes the fashion, he will always find a way to justify it.

4) In relation to certain germinating errors, he has a declared sympathy, or at the very least is neutral in face of them. For example, as regards Communism, he is against it from the start; but as for Socialism, which is nothing more than a candy coated form of Communism, he says, "We need to concede something." In the end he accommodates himself. If he ever reacts against evil, his reaction is timid and discreet. Nothing is more amusing than to watch a liberal Catholic reprimanding his child, a student, or an employee. Let us say an employee commits a bad mistake and the liberal Catholic calls him in and says, "Friend, I have been so good to you.... Have I not bent over backwards to help you.... Please do not do this again. Besides, it is for your own good that I do this because this mistake

will only hurt you." The employee gives three lame excuses as to why he did it, to which the liberal Catholic, if he is a bit more energetic, might respond, "Listen, you need to give me a better reason than that." This is a very easy-going Catholic.

A true Catholic is anti-egalitarian

Here we have two well-defined attitudes. What characterises a truly fervent Catholic soul, according to the degrees of spiritual life, is that he holds the Catholic religion and all its teaching as a supreme value. We have proven that a hierarchical and anti-egalitarian vision of the Universe is part and parcel of those teachings.

Now the revolutionary movement of our days holds egalitarianism as its supreme value. Hence, the only attitude of a true Catholic vis-á-vis this whole egalitarian movement today is to be diametrically opposed to it.

Tradition, Family and Property Association (TFP)

A SCHOOL OF THOUGHT. As a civic association of Catholics, TFP bases itself on the teachings of the traditional magisterium of the Roman Catholic Church. We see the crisis of contemporary society as having its roots in the most profound problems of the soul of present-day man, whence it spread to his whole personality and to all his activities. We understand this crisis to include:

1. A loss of Faith and a rejection of the principles of the natural order established by God.

2. The continuous opposition of the disorderly passions of the soul, particularly pride and sensuality, to the mandates of Natural and Moral Law, leading to absolute equality and licentiousness.

3. The existence of a process, through which individuals—and even whole nations—are gradually attracted either to the pole of good and of order, or else to the pole of evil and disorder.

A SCHOOL OF ACTION. To counter the above revolutionary process, which led to the present anti-Christian order of things, we aim to re-establish Christian civilisation. To accomplish this we use every available peaceful and lawful means, such as:

Direct action to inform the public about key ideological issues, thereby frequently changing the course of events. In public campaigns that are a hallmark of the TFP, our volunteers talk directly to people on the streets and hand out leaflets. To date we have distributed approximately 2 million leaflets in this way.

Informing and educating through leaflets, newsletters and books dealing with a range of topics of interest to Catholics and the general public. TFP's carefully researched books and position papers always receive the highest praise for their accuracy and in-depth insights into issues. *TFP Viewpoint*, our bimonthly newsletter, keeps us in touch with our friends. We also give talks to a wide variety of groups, explaining our work, or dealing with specific topics.

Why Tradition, Family, Property?

Why is it important to defend tradition, the family and the right to private property? At first sight these values might seem to be an arbitrary mix. But, in fact, they are three pillars supporting every sound civilisation, and especially Christian civilisation. Abolish any one of them and the other two will wither and die. They are values rooted in both Natural Law and Divine Revelation. Today they are under attack as never before. To restore Christian civilisation we must foster and defend tradition, the family and the principle of private property.

Tradition is the sum of a people's accomplishments in the religious, moral, cultural and material fields. It is a gift handed down from generation to generation by virtue of which youth moves forward with a surer step, enlightened and guided by the experience of elders. Tradition is not merely an historic value, nor simply a romantic yearning for bygone days. It is an indispensable factor for contemporary life. Through tradition societies avoid stagnation, as well as chaos and revolt.

Family is tradition's most dynamic element. If the family did not exist, neither would tradition, for families are the bearers of natural and supernatural moral values that are passed on from one generation to the next. A family must develop this rich patrimony into a school of being, living, progressing and serving one's country and Christendom. Otherwise it risks producing maladjusted individuals who don't know who they are and who cannot stably and logically fit into any social group.

Property is a human right based on the nature of man as a free individual entitled to the fruits of his labour. Private property is indispensable for the well-being of the family. In accordance with their God-given instincts, all parents worthy of the name work, struggle and save to provide a secure future for their children. Thus, families accumulate patrimonies which are passed on from generation to generation as inheritance. Inheritance is the rendezvous of family and property. Although even more important than material possessions are intangible goods like education and cultural and moral values. To deny the legitimacy of this is to make parents strangers to their own children. The seventh and ninth Commandments explicitly state the sacredness of private property.

The destruction of tradition, the family, and private property has been sought by all the totalitarian movements of the modern age, especially Socialism, National Socialism (Nazism), Fascism and Communism. These movements are natural enemies of Christian civilisation.

Who is Plinio Corrêa de Oliveira?

PROF. PLINIO CORRÊA DE OLIVEIRA was born in 1908 in São Paulo, Brazil, a country having the largest Catholic population in the world. Both his parents came from traditional aristocratic families.

He dedicated his life to promoting the cause of the Catholic Church and Christian civilisation. In 1928 he joined the Marian Congregations, then Brazil's largest Catholic movement, soon rising to national leadership, and distinguishing himself as an orator, lecturer and man of action. At twenty-four years of age he was elected to the Brazilian Constitutional Assembly of 1933 as a candidate for the Catholic Electoral League.

In the following years he practiced law, held the chair of history of civilisation at the University of São Paulo Law School, and the chair of modern and contemporary history at the Pontifical Catholic University of São Paulo. In 1960 he founded the Brazilian Society for the Defence of Tradition,

Family and Property, serving as its president until his death in 1995.

As a thinker and writer, Professor Corrêa de Oliveira made a major contribution to modern Catholic thought. An

avowed Thomist, he was the author of 15 books and over 2,500 in-depth essays and articles. His works include: *In Defence of Catholic Action, Revolution and Counter-Revolution, The Church and the Communist State: The Impossible Coexistence, Nobility and Analogous Traditional Elites in the Allocutions of Pius XII* and many others.

While president of the São Paulo Archdiocesan Board of Catholic Action, he directed the weekly *Legionário*, making it Latin America's front-ranking Catholic newspaper. Later, he was a contributor to the influential monthly magazine Catolicismo, and a syndicated columnist with Brazil's largest daily newspaper, the *Folha de São Paulo*.

Professor Corrêa de Oliveira's life and work was the inspiration for other Catholics around the world to establish TFPs in their respective countries. His legacy is seen today in the thriving school of thought he founded and in his worldwide following of disciples. ■

This work was finished on
19th March 2011,
The Solemnity of St. Joseph

For further information
and publications:

Tradition, Family, Property Association
P.O. Box 2713 – Glasgow G62 6YJ
Tel: 0141-956-7391 – Fax: 0141-956-6978
email: info@tfpuk.org.uk